GODDESS OF DEMOCRACY

GODDESS OF DEMOCRACY

an occupy lyric

HENRY WEI LEUNG

OMNIDAWN PUBLISHING
OAKLAND, CALIFORNIA
2017

Cover image: *Absent of Speech*, Yip Kin Bon, 2014/2015,
190 x 120 cm, newspaper. www.yipkinbon.com

Cover and interior set in Kabel LT Std and Didot LT Std
Chinese characters set in Menlo and Apple LiSung

Cover and interior design by Gillian Olivia Blythe Hamel

Offset printed in the United States
by Edwards Brothers Malloy, Ann Arbor, Michigan
On 55# Enviro Natural 100% Recycled 100% PCW
Acid Free Archival Quality FSC Certified Paper

Library of Congress Cataloging-in-Publication Data

Names: Leung, Henry W., author.
Title: Goddess of democracy : an occupy lyric / Henry Wei Leung.
Description: Oakland, California : Omnidawn Publishing, 2017.
Identifiers: LCCN 2017020695 | ISBN 9781632430403 (paperback : alk. paper)
Classification: LCC PS3612.E9214 A6 2017 | DDC 811/.6--dc23
LC record available at https://lccn.loc.gov/2017020695

Published by Omnidawn Publishing, Oakland, California
www.omnidawn.com   (510) 237-5472   (800) 792-4957
10 9 8 7 6 5 4 3 2 1
ISBN: 978-1-63243-040-3

*for [   ] ***

for your freedom

"We are like Ulysses who had been carried away during his sleep by sailors and woke in a strange land, longing for Ithaca with a longing that rent his soul. Suddenly Athena opened his eyes and he saw that he was in Ithaca."

SIMONE WEIL

"I'm there already, I must be there already, perhaps I'm not alone, perhaps a whole people is here, and the voice its voice, coming to me fitfully, we would have lived, been free a moment ..."

SAMUEL BECKETT

CONTENTS

IV. NEITHER SELF NOR NOT-SELF NOR BOTH NOR NEITHER

ENVOI AT LOW TIDE

INTRODUCTION

Henry W. Leung's *Goddess of Democracy: an Occupy lyric* is a powerful poetics on civil disobedience. The core subject in his debut is the titular Goddess of Democracy, the 33-foot paper-mache statue that was first built and then razed during the 1989 Tiananmen Square massacre. Leung directly addresses the Goddess and her replicas throughout the book while bearing witness to the 2014 Umbrella Revolution that paralyzed Hong Kong for 79 days. Although the narrator appears to have been there, documenting the uprising, he also acknowledges his unease as witness since he is not a "native" but one who returns to China after growing up in the States. I love this book because Leung doesn't give us an accessible individualized account to pull at the American reader's heartstrings but instead uses his first-hand insights to interrogate Western ideologies of democracy: "what is freedom when divorced from *from?*"

The book tracks the narrator's fragmentary consciousness as he dips in and out of the actual uprising. The voice is both impassioned and detached, coalescing into prose passages or atomizing into words scattered on the page. The I is not Whitman's monumental I who contains multitudes but an I "torn off" into throng, an I who both belongs and doesn't belong to the assembled we. His poetry reminds me of Myung Mi Kim's fragments or George Oppen's lyric that searches for a constructive encounter with the crowd. Lately, many Americans are finally awake and thinking of disobedience. Leung not only documents disobedience, but historicizes it, turns it to a global question, and asks what comes after. *Goddess of Democracy: an Occupy lyric* is a necessary and inspiring read.

Cathy Park Hong
2017

I

NEITHER DONKEY NOR HORSE

PREAMBLE: ROOM FOR CADAVERS

I reach in to palm your heart:
three decades dead and still the same
grease-yellow as the plastic napkins
layered here to keep your organs moist.
I never thought we came apart like this,
like sheet, like blanket, pillow after pillow
unpeeled by morning, trace of warmth
where once a body swelled.

Buttons plug your joints from leaks,
your fat scooped out, tufts of ribs tattered
like spoiled meat—I have eaten so much
of this before this
    this one flesh

        this stainless steel
            blue damp towel
                dear body open

let me swallow destination

but let me leave with nothing
like you on my greased

gloved hands

no piece seeping through
to show my maze and mean—

don't ever fold my soft bones back.
I'm just the floor of an ocean receding,
a soft rubble seeding nothing.

I have seen nothing yet.

But I have known heat
enough in the lover's breath
and cough at night.

I have known bodies.

LIFE SENTENCES SONNET FOR THE GODDESS

Tiananmen Square, June 1989

1

You were born in papier-mâché, a face plastered white, a thirty-three foot emolument on the fourth day, facing the portrait of the Chairman of Mao.

2

Father died that year we snuck through Hong Kong for San Francisco you were not the Statue of Liberty we landed in the great quake.

3

Nushen, "goddess" – not far from *nusheng*, "schoolgirl" – your hair cropped like Mother's – like that girl ruling masses from a megaphone – her skinny hand pocketed – her four abortions.

4

And wasn't I the forgery of a body never meant, never mine, never mind, so that someone in the rubble would forever look like me?

5

Goddess, your body was expedited from the body of a man leaning on a pole, flipped upright. Severed, his pole became your torch.

6

Some people have stared at heaven's gate for decades waiting for a sign. Some people settled, and settle for seams.

7

A tank severed your hand, then the rest. You reemerged in harder mediums in tourist troves, where I was taught to lust for image, just images.

8

I fell in love with love's treasons. Which of these remain forbidden words: *goddess, swallow, roam, freedom, I*?

9

G.O.D. in Hong Kong means Goods of Desire, a fashion brand which sounds like *jyu hou di*: "live better." Does anyone say "God" except at first mistaken sight? Goddess of—

10

One day, my heartbeat quit its symmetry. An EKG said A.Fib and asked if I'd had heart attacks before this? I died of—

11

A place can be a people, just as grammar is the making of a religion. Why does this language only desire nouns and noun states and not move? Body of—

12

Listen: that year we were two eggs from one hen, dipped in black ink. We were thrown at the portrait of the Chairman of Mao. A thunderstorm washed us clean, washing the aberration.

13

But I've never had heart failure. But the machines insist. The machines insist.

14

What I mean is: we were the aberration. What I mean is: *Let me be your country. Let me be nothing for you.*

DISOBEDIENCE

On 31 Aug 2014, Beijing announced its terms for universal suffrage in the special administrative region of Hong Kong. A massive rally was organized that same night, initiating the oncoming months of civil disobedience.

I myself have been here:
been a hollowing throng of sweat
hoping for a name
or blessing, been among the lonely
solidaire offstage
banking on a harbor breeze;
I have been the weft
and tangle
of a mother's lilt I can't
unhear from your cries raised.

I stood among and gave you
neither stay nor shore nor help
from rain. I stood inside
a silent night of cell phone lights
with all my hands
hanging. For the record
I told the foreigners nothing
when asked. I looked
like someone to ask.

I've barely arrived
after birth
and migration, a body
dismantled of time,
waking in words, shaking
a paper lung.

I was not meant to survive.
So forgive my participation.
Forgive me my love for freedom

and for my foreign question: what is
    freedom when divorced from
        from?

I am one child, two dialects.
I am an overseas democracy
with Chinese characteristics.
I am the bridge and long road
of blank votes, proof of
having been, of having
been more
than shopping.

I am ardor

for a hostage here
too wise to hear,
who lay down her hands
on my knuckles
as a beatitude promising

the freedom of no escape.

She knows no comers
promise solace;
she herself was there
for the five thousand
exterminations.

And I squat here
on loamy sidewalk stone
where a ragged dog has lain to rest
with such an effort of dignity
that when the time comes
to hose us down,
who will say

which of us is decay
and which the sculpture of it?

ISLAND OF THE GODDESS

On 28 Sep 2014, tear gas was launched at a peaceful protest led by university students in Hong Kong. They had only their umbrellas with which to defend themselves.

During the Occupy campaign that followed, the Goddess of Democracy replica at Chinese University was left hooded with a black garbage bag over her face.

██████ [ ] ██████████

When did I leave the country of want

Handprints of stars cup the rain
You can't buy love but you can buy flower

Mister where is the forgiven city

A skin waves from the column
Garden hose of the heart

Mister where is the triumphant statue

Cemented at the knees
Down by water

[   ] ██ ██████████

7 means dick
71 means handover remember

689 means broadly representative functional constituency
689 means chief executive so 7689 means

852 means hong kong people

922 means student strike 928 means tear gas
1003 means police thug collusion remember

8964 means tanks remember goddess remember

也 ■■■■■■■

What equality taught you such a shame
For rising above sameness

Dream of sevenths key of F / No tonic

Some ribbons are a dangling infinity
Some shades insoluble

Caught between light / And absence

What becomes of revolution
When you wake from the rain

Flushed among strangers / No enemies

What can you tell the old loneliness
Your bed bisects a barricade

[   ]■啦][   ]

You plead for more bodies

Liberty Village / Agora Admiralty

Umbrella Plaza / Study Corner / Pokémon Centre

Faith Street / Resistance Ave / Democracy Way / Long Road

Shall we always be longing / Stay

Sound of water between stones
Highway rat between tents
Mosquito in the supplicant's cowl

Black hole home

There are no citizens
In a prayer's city

Some cities build paper houses

Just to burn / Then hose the asphalt down
Flowers for the dead

Rent so high even corpses can't stay
Polluted sun peeling

Recycled people / Yell into a wall
Great wall of SARS
Great wall of milk powder
Great wall of toilet squatters baby border rushers
Great wall empire plopped on a rooftop
Great wall white ghost colony nostalgia

Brick wall with glass wings

███████ ██   ]

To vote from Freedom Quarter

Late night diaspora sweats
Exile dread

Tear gassed is no credential
Pepper sprayed is no credential
Interviewed by BBC is no credential

Yellow ribbon blue ribbon no ribbon
Straight white males can be cared for
Cigarette butt doused in tea

Sawed-off water bottle
Shall we hold

We hollow torso writhing
To catch the light

Doesn't every flag bow
Like a broken canopy

If the statue of the goddess
Is hooded as if for execution

If a bus abandoned
Becomes a democracy wall

If we sculpt a rain-shield
For the streetlamps' yellow fire

If we plant flowers in a bottle
If it takes this much violence

Gases stuck where breath

If words are not enough
If horror in the bloom

If happy birthday
If highways / If aloe / If orchid

What if advertisement will not save us
What if freedom just means shopping

Construction beams
Swivel like rifle arms

Someone drops shit and cricket bags
Someone pours down kerosene

Our shoes sticky for days

Captain America joins Mong Kok
Helps us hold the line

Grievous / *Tricolore cockade*
Buzzsaw altar boltcutter altar

This is *Pok*-Head Square

Arguing Arena Agon Ground Zero
Attack dogs muzzled at Yet Honest Road

Cap gets arrested shield confiscated
That night Spider-Man appears

The crowd goes wild

Some of us without parents all month
Some for years and years and years

Freedom hangs a pink sneaker
From a pink awning

And Lennon sings a world without context

█████████ 乜係乜

When I brought the whole pig to my grandmother's new grave I stepped over the stone of my father's but didn't know it the name was so small the weeds so long so beautiful

How to write the word for *revolution* you flay a pig's carcass lengthwise hang the organs from a hook you wash and wash until the cool lard shakes

Then next to it write *fate*

[█████████]

Already one month of endangered speech
游 & 里 UP

Dear empire one
Meow meow meow

Dear empire two
The beeble say remember revise rename

Dear empire one-half
What is language extinction

Incense / Pillar
Crumbling ash

Aunties bring red birthday eggs
Our fingers glow through the night

27

Isn't there a death grip on the grail
Isn't it called compromise

Isn't its guardian an agony of stone
Won't it yield to the first who says

Tell me how you've suffered I'm listening

Like abalone and a grain of sand
Scrubbing the concave mirror

Flower in a bottle

Armed tank of recycled plastic
We know the promised end

What is the sound of jade bells breaking

What is genuine suffrage fidelity to law fatalism arrest

What is the self the terrible acquired thing

We were given half an eloquence too many ifs

We know freedom compromises blood for time

We body politic we drumline pulse

We last person plural

We hold

BRIDGE   IN

June   :
         :
July   :
August   :
         :
         :
         :
         :
September   :
         :
         :

October   :
         :   violence
         :   built
         :   built
         :
         :
         :
         :
         :   **hung**
         :
November   :
         :
         :   **the agon**

                                        agora
                                         orpheum

I leaned against a sycamore and peeled it to paper when a dying person called me instead of an ambulance. Sobbing and listening to sobbing are separate skills. The dry voice at the end is like a dusk sky turning sick shades of green. "Who have I suffered for?" To delay another's death, I told a lifetime's worth of lies and promises. A passing dog bit my shin, the most foreign of my limbs. The wound was not deep, yet it remains. A deeper wound would be like absence. I have not mastered absence. I walk along rivers pocketing stones. I cannot bear myself in. I need a volcano, a swallowing like a door without a doorway.

{♠}

A banner : 我
要
真
普
選

When all but the top is torn off, what remains? "I."* And above it, a symbol. I've moved and moved, but from every sublet, from each butchered bedroom, I can see a smokestack, a crematorium across the way. My latest window stands between a pillow and a highway. Cars shake up the dice in me, my sum unsettled. Some nights I wander in dry weather raising a yellow umbrella. Sometimes someone yells at me to die. *Someone* is the fourth-person pronoun. I ask someone which is harder, true love or true suffrage, and someone is unsettled. Eventually, the I is torn off.

* (My translation.)

GOODS OF DEMOCRACY

Theseus built the first democracy,
a cult of two bodies—
Aphrodite Pandemos and Peitho:
desire and *persuasion*.
Peitho was the wife of Hermes,
so throw in winged correspondence
and a tourist underworld, too,
pillar of salt wind mistaken for want.

Back then, in a honey dearth
a girl was sent to slaughter
an ox, beat its corpse
to softness, then leave it shedded
for the new year.

From the body: bees.
From the one: many.

I loved an aphrodite once
who rock-climbed without arms
like drift smoke in a dark mouth—
I wrote her to the second cloth,
from eros to error, sprayed crowns
on painted names
we couldn't sustain—
slender omen, my venus
and *venenum*.

I tried to be the unnamed symbol
on the walls before the buzzing,
when horns and bones and hair
resembled still-unbroken road.
I tried to map a person
like an aubade
with no lines set down,
raised to heaven as is.

But maybe love is best indifferent.
Democracy, too. *Metaxu*:
the force that cleaves us

is the force we cleave to,
double-surfaced thin transparency,
mirror in a daylit window, freed

and for free

and for nothing.
Isn't privation

a proof of love?
Persuasion

is a wilderness
arguing on a street corner

almost near home.

PORTSMOUTH SQUARE,
SAN FRANCISCO CHINATOWN

G.O.D. replica raised in 1994

For here there is no man
who ever sees you, goddess
holding up a city's lint
on a pigeon on a dry
bronze torch, goddess over
tic-tac-toe playpens, goddess
of buying, drinking, liberty,
oblivion, of the onion skin
of stale sunlight, deep song
of void between one flag
lowered and another raised.

Here is no man who sees
your invisible days.
I see the plaster-white drip
from your temple
to your cheek, a peeling
like a second skin
in an age of birds shitting
on this golden port
of wandering in a wandering
long without rain,
in this refuge, this refuse
of waterbound dreams.

Goddess, walk backward with me.

Step back into the fire that refines
and be refined, be molded
by hands like oars, be more
than those corporate, other
goddesses, those empty-sleeved
epoxy-soaked cloaks like
steeples looming, birds
nesting in their hollow hoods,

be more—for above
your banks these muses hang
like an old dream left behind
in another foreign room.

VICTIMS OF COMMUNISM MEMORIAL, WASHINGTON, D.C.

G.O.D. replica raised in 2007

You oversee traffic from a corner
where timed lights leave all things equal
between Chinatown and Capitol Hill,

where a low heaven's gargoyle
blinks and records, where oceanic
tongues unthread your temple.

Someone slats a name between
the roof supports for *goddess* and for
victim, for the coming storm,

and cuts away from stone a perfect
thing, then rubs it smooth, a thing
meant to survive the things of us.

But in the chiseling did they find
a David—that Abrahamic trick—
or just the same hard earth divided?

I remember floating like a desert
in a box on the sea, where to see
a coming storm was to see the land

erasing: a perfection; and perfection
could not save us and the storm is
always coming and I sing the storm.

I sweat at your feet in a gulp of smoke
released, a halo of solitude, counting up
old receipts, a victim too of communism's

cheap memorials. We are the cobweb
shaking loose on sideview mirrors,
the clock tower pining, the empty quiver.

Armed Freedom oversees us model
minorities from her dome of old fasces.
Goddess, you must change your life.

You are only as dark as bronze,
exactly as blank as desired.
Goddess, burn my pockets whole.

Give me paired zeroes like blind eyes,
like infinity, like truth without malice.
Goddess, capitalize my death to death.

Let us feed on love and not on food.
Let us feed on a love for food,
on love for food we'll never eat.

II

NEITHER DEATH NOR LIFE NOR ANGELS

AN UMBRELLA: MOVEMENT

Who is in love with no one. *Who* is the fifth-person pronoun. *No one* is the sixth. Imagine an impossible love, like an impossible grammar. Who protests a longing for no one. No one tries to hide from love. What is it to embrace a suffering street? Is it in the nature of protest to turn inward? Someone became a wooden face. Who wept behind the mask. No one was a symbol. And the sea, the night sea.

{☂}
我

The body vanishes. Who is not free. No one is not free. An other is not the seventh-person pronoun. The people is not the seventh-person pronoun. There are no more pronouns: only anonymity. It was like writing letters from a rooftop from which many had jumped before me. Suddenly I realized that not belonging in the world is not enough. I did not belong in two worlds, perhaps three. I let each letter fall, great post of gray trees. Perhaps loneliness can well so deep that it becomes joy.

as
Paper   pen
and

"   **Love**   "

ember   in
a
cup

to
be

to
be

to

rot

I

face
a
smashed
lit
cup   "   "
lost

ember   in   a
bog
shed for   you

TRANSLATION POEM FOR HONG KONG

To mime a more exacting fire

In which I translate the other
Despite *I was there* I was there too

A flag an encounter with silence

A man giving and giving his river of kerosene
To the long road of protest
Why can't I light students on fire

In which please translate my cigarette
Beneath armored police on a galleon stage

Three men sail into a city of no citizenship
With a megaphone, a gas of tears, and a camcorder

Red light blinking at the end of the tunnel

The other way the other telling

《最後通牒》
此致土匪路霸，你們霸佔道路，
非法集會，已有十多天了，嚴重
阻礙全港九市民的正常生活，學
生不能上課，父母不能返工，家
庭收入大減，商店沒有生意，快
要結束營業了，你們的愚蠢佔領
行動，是雙重犯法，天怒人怨，
令到社會與家庭破裂，父母傷心
。現限令你們在十月二十日晚上
十一時十四分之前自行撤退，否
則請你們吃屎尿墨水彈，你們吃
飽了就要回家睡覺吧。
全體愛港的市民，我們一齊合作
每人做十個臭水彈，送給他們作
為晚餐吧，此彈清湯有特效！
臭水彈用屎十尿十墨水，一個橙
的份量，用薄膠袋紮住袋口就成
保家救香港大聯盟

"ULTIMATUM"
Respectfully Dear Brigand Road-Hogs
tyrannically occupying roads, illegally
assembling for over ten days with grave
consequence to the lives of Hong Kong Island/
Kowloon's citizens, students can't go to
school, parents can't go to work, household
incomes subtracting, store incomes subtracting—
your foolish Occupy campaign is doubly criminal,
spreading discontent ["the sky's rage the people's complaint"]

A thousand copies of this white note flitting down

A dark apartment window in a billboard-lit darkness

A protest camp staring at stars dislodged, lit up in wonder

One morning I passed a man weeping though his cheeks were dry

An insect of iridescent hue trampled in the [   ] of the night before

Dm stands for Deemocrycee

> *rupturing society and the home, aggrieving parents.*
> *You must withdraw by 20 October at 11:14pm,*

"Fourteen" sounds like "certain death"

> *otherwise you'll be invited to eat shit-urine*
> *ink bombs, of which you can have your fill*
> *and then go home to sleep, okay?*
> *All citizens who love Hong Kong,*
> *let's make ten cloacal bombs as gifts*
> *for their dinner, an especially enriching bomb consommé!*
> *These bombs are a [learned] dark ink*
> *+ shit*
> *+ piss*
> *weight of orange*

Language is a darkness interpreted

> *made of thin plastic bags tied at the mouth*

> *Allied Federation Coalition League of Family Protectors*
> *Hong Kong Saviors*

44

[my translation]

Tied at the mouth

Sweeping

ISLAND OF THE GODDESS

On 25 Nov, 11 Dec, and 15 Dec 2014, crackdowns were coordinated by the police
to demolish the three Umbrella protest camps. The reaction to the first of these was
a "mobile" Occupy, which went on nightly for years.

i

What they meant by give the people
back their streets was let the vast
machines back in, this city grinding
gears inside the garden
in the animal in me.

I remain years behind, years
as in wandering, insoluble
nostos. I never meant
to this world; I am not meaning,
not promise, not time. I can't
even promise myself:
what I own is not I.
Indifferent anthem
of the sun.

In the agon, after demolition:
      ghost town swept by cops
           where color is a contraband

ii

How will it be
to be human again?
I've been to such silences
as a sudden flag
embracing its pole,
where I saw hollow bodies
multiply like bells. I know
a fire wishes me well.

The hides split open, yes.
I surrendered half a life's anger, yes.
I surrendered solace, too.

In the agora, after demolition:
      a post-it, a democracy dog,
            and a congregation

            iii
Did holding hands in the rain
change the nature of rain?
Four kids kick a ball on a field
so vast that one falls asleep
in a goal made of netting.
Wilderness is something else here.
It's one trombone against a world's
traffic, lyre of a ribcage
rumbling and flayed.

I am a grotesque
mouthpiece now, but you
wouldn't know it: they
keep scrubbing me clean.

In the orpheum, after demolition:
      a hooded speaker fights for volume
            against the old freedom ballad

sung nearby for small change.

            iiii
The earth was an eggshell
full of black hole.
The sense of belonging

left a trauma on the body.
It was the body's last trauma.

Here was a thing that changed my life:
I stood inside the calm eye of a storm
with wings enough to set the gates free.

The eggshell swallowed the storm.
Language blew out like a sleeve.

This city—kissed by a chimera,
and even I spend my best years
in a golden future's cage.

I myself have seen a gnawed
and abandoned bleached pelican
skeleton where a sea had left
thousands of blue jelly velella discs
like fingerprints peeling on the beach—
dislocated wing, lost beak, neck
bowed forward to a missing gut and
wreathed in moss, translucent spine
carried to another face of rock.
Above, the cliffs were sculpted by
ten thousand longings without us.
You told me to take anything,
take everything from you. But
if the world had one less mountain,
then even time and the malady
of love would change: change,
that parasite bursting its dark ink
inside our windows, swallowing
our holes. We never could live up
to fiction, always did love
wrongly, always wrong to want
a better world at the expense
of the world. Maybe it's enough
to save a life just by seeing it
and seeming unafraid. You know
I'd be repulsed by my whirling
in this world if I had elsewhere
to turn. Remember that old grotto
paradise which no man leaves
unfulfilled, or ever finds again?
Let us die with our stomachs.
There is only this world.

DEAR EXILE

Two ways I can cross this street:
one in which you're at arm's reach,

another where I turn and trust
the world to roll each ocean

in between us. They unrequite
our names—bittermelon gate,

far shore that sates—and wrought
from us a kind of grace, a kinder rot:

that *I am nothing in your world now*.
I wish you nothing-wishes, wholeness

as you are. May I find a way through
to your pain, but not to take it from you.

May I never take from you again.
May you tunnel inward, break even—

and become just what you are: miracle
without solace, burned and invisible

firefly heaving a burden of light,
your silences freed but misaligned.

Didn't we take the poison, we invocation,
we spring debris forgotten by seasons,

we art, we hour of night, lost, veering
to freedom, we windchill not carrying

their cold but only heat's absence,
we singeing, skinned matchhead—

we signed that archipelago.

So bear me away too.
And unbear me in you.

ARCHERY FOR A FUTURE DAUGHTER

The great bow pointing down suggests a bullseye in the earth.

A hole in the earth would go perfectly through.

Is that fecundity, or terror?

You hunger for air, you draw and draw, and bow becomes doorjamb.

But who is straight enough to be the arrow?

Everyone I know is round and unanswerable.

Is the string empty because unnotched, lacking figure and direction?

Love could be a figure, and direction.

Only, like the sun, it would stop at face and recurve, leaving emptiness outlined.

There are other kinds of bows:

Bows to mean burdened, sloping shoulders, and boats;

Bows to unravel;

Bows drawn sideways and acoustic.

For a cello, for instance, emptiness is all.

What music would we leave if not hollow-bodied?

To know even this may make being more bearable.

But you, love, are an apostrophe: you never asked to be borne.

III

RUINS ABOVE WATER

Jan 2015

The Independent called it the "Umbrella Revolution." Imagine that: the name came from English-language voyeurism first before being translated back into Chinese for the protest camps. It's a name that's still contentious with those who insist on "Umbrella Movement" instead. "Revolution" was romantic and provocational. It paved a road for mainland Chinese newspapers to declare the "defeat of Hong Kong's color revolution" in December. And if such will be China's official history, then like a thousand other incidents and suppressions it is an erasure of individual experience. But unlike those thousand others, this erasure was already in place at the beginning, on September 28, with a name stamped on by foreign press, with Hong Kong's story told by its colonizers again.

In October, Kenny G visited the protest camp in Admiralty. He was the first American celebrity to do so. By then, signs had already been hung up, reading, "This is Not a Tourist Attraction," and, "No Photo Please! Here Is Not Zoo." Kenny G took a photo of himself grinning in front of some tents, and posted this on his website. China issued a warning about foreign interference, with an intimation of him losing sales in the mainland. He replaced the photo with an apology, a note with love for China, and a platitude for peaceful resolution. Like most protest tourists, he didn't understand that to cross from the sidewalk into the threshold of occupied streets was to join in what the government had declared an illegal gathering. It would be civil disobedience. Of course it's possible that a bumbling foreigner might trip over an activity about which he knows nothing. But failing to understand is a sorry excuse.

In November, in the lull, I was sometimes asked to guide people in a tour of the camps, people I barely knew. I never did. I never could. Such a tour would have to be an act of intimacy, a tour into myself. Would you give a stranger a tour of your home, of your private joys and traumas? Would you give a stranger a tour of someone else's home? People wanted to understand. Yet I can't help remembering the Americans I met, who told me with a perversely excited pride just after they had arrived, that finally, *finally*, they understood what it meant to be a minority. They were quick to forget that privilege transfers, that being foreign is not the same as being made invisible, and that understanding is not a checklist of pains or conquests. I graduated from a private university in the States, where I lived with kids who owned Porsches and horses and who, for one day a year, volunteered to subsist on food stamps. I grew up on food stamps. These were some of the same kids who would go on to be voluntourists, writers and photographers and artisans of other people's pain.

In November, Zhou Fengsuo visited the protest camps. He was active at Tiananmen in 1989, and is still high on China's wanted list. He arrived from California, and took photos of himself in the encampment. What made him different from a Kenny G? Before he left for Taiwan, he gave a short farewell talk beside the Umbrella Plaza stage. Only about fifteen of us stood by to listen while a light rain fell. Several times he stopped and turned his face away to recollect himself. He was one of the only outsiders I heard whose refrain was not the usual, "Let's all hate China," but that very rare, "Let's all love Hong Kong." He was asked big China questions by the audience, and he kept emphasizing: democracy in China is not the responsibility of Hong Kong; injustice in China is not the responsibility of Hong Kong. He understood deeply what it meant to see a protest for itself, to see it unnamed and as it is.

The real difference might be in a private moment of his which I witnessed by accident. I was finishing a meal outside the canteen at Hong Kong University where the Pillar of Shame stands: a red tornado of a sculpture with distorted, emaciated, pained figures bulging out from its mass, as though from a single body stripped of flesh. It is a memorial for the Tiananmen Massacre. I've spent a whole adolescence sitting by monuments ignored and covered in bird shit; I once watched tourists kneel down by the Goddess of Democracy replica in San Francisco, just to frame a photo from a low angle — worse, to frame it with the TransAmerica building (also called Pereira's

Prick) towering over the Goddess—and then leave without taking those three extra steps to read what she was meant to be a memory of. But what Zhou did that day I've never seen at any monument anywhere. He crossed into the field of pebbles surrounding the Pillar, and looked carefully at the unsteady threshold beneath his feet. He circled the Pillar, then kneeled. He reached forward. He pressed his hand against the bodies there.

[2]

I never had the right to live as I do, and the story of my illegal birth in China is one I keep revising in my rememberings. I was cut from a seam and hidden on the other side of the ocean. Freedom is just such a thing: revision and imagination. It is the permission that we give ourselves to live, despite the world we live in.

But responsibility is something else. I'm here on a Fulbright grant, which means I could be proof of foreign interference in the protests. My views and actions do not reflect those of the U.S. Department of State. If umbrellas are in fact contraband, then arrest me and deport me and revoke my funding now. If uniformed men dwarfed by the shadows of their helmets appear at my door one night, I'll go without regret, quoting an old Gym Class Heroes lyric: "I love my life. Bitches."

But responsibility is still something else. I never told my family here what I was up to. They never supported the protests. They knew at once that danger went beyond tear gas and rifles and shotguns, that in this country and in their lives a security camera blinking in the night sufficed. The worries of responsibility slide sideways. To face this is to face your loved ones across the great wall of a dinner table. Responsibility is anonymous, unnamed, is an invisible suffering which shakes up everyone at your shoulders and in the end merits nothing. It is to stand sweating at China Customs on the way to see my uncle in the mainland, unsure if the white terror of ID checks in Mong Kok had at last caught up to me, if my face had been traced into a system and a stranger behind the screen of a vast machinery had given me a better name.

I can't declare myself "for" or "against." These two words are as useless as "us" and "them" in the face of understanding, in the face of all our failures to understand each other. If you ever complained to me about the protests and how those people were a spoiled and irrational bunch, I stopped listening because you weren't talking about human beings; you were gossiping about objects. "They" is not singular. Human sympathy is not public opinion. Unliking a movement doesn't unburden anyone of it. A fourteen-year-old girl arrested for drawing flowers in chalk on a wall is not a hashtag or an idea. She has a name and it is not Chalk Girl. As early as October, Ah Lung was struck in the tailbone by riot police and permanently paralyzed from the waist down. You can still find him in his wheelchair on Mong Kok's sidewalks some nights, where the mobile form of Occupy still goes on nightly. He never received recompense or even acknowledgment, because the authorities claimed he was genetically predisposed to paralysis. His status was reported regularly from Umbrella Plaza, but his story never made it to big English media. A professor here told me later, "Well, nobody's been hurt yet." I explained about Ah Lung. This professor's first reaction was: "But that's such a common name, Ah Lung."

There is a history of erasure here for which privilege is responsible. English is one such privilege. Who controls naming in a place where the language of power is not the language spoken by the people? Who will caption the forces of a movement and, more, who will take responsibility for it?

Among the miracles of my life, I count the privilege of translating an essay by local fiction writer Hon Lai Chu. She wrote it from grief after the Mong Kok crackdown in November, and I read it after the Admiralty camp was destroyed in December. I stood by as the study corner at the heart of Umbrella Plaza—the very locus of a peaceful and diligent protest—was picked up by indifferent machines, then folded and crushed alongside water-filled barriers which were also lifted and squeezed dry. I felt like I was losing a home that had never been mine to begin with. The sight left me broken for weeks. The first part of the miracle was to find, in Hon's words, the articulation of what I myself had had no words for; the second part of the miracle was to be able to give words back, to be the lyre of someone else's song. As my translation formed alongside the original, something unclenched inside me and I broke down sobbing. Perhaps that's the promise of translation, the beginning of understanding: you reach your hand out to a foreign body and discover that it is yours too. The words are your own after all.

But it's not enough. This will not do. Will it mean anything to an English readership when I say that the title, "I Just Want to See the Sea," has a light rhyme and alliteration in Cantonese, but not in Mandarin? All you'll know is: "Translated from the Chinese." But there are at least three Chineses in Hong Kong and two of them are being erased. The first is a written Traditional Chinese read aloud in Cantonese; it's the Chinese of the writers, musicians, newscasters, government officials. But it's now being filtered out: schools receive extra subsidies when they teach "Chinese" in the mainland's Mandarin instead, effectively translating all text into a foreign tongue. And then there's the Cantonese you hear on the street, with its own systematic grammar and a unique written form, made up of Chinese lexica, Roman alphanumerics, and recently even emoji. Not only is this not taught in school, but it's dismissed, it's vulgar. In fact, it's the mother tongue. No wonder that in a campaign for suffrage and dignity in the face of an encroaching Chinese empire, many of the protest signs were very distinctly Cantonese, resisting translation. And so what is it to be translated simply "from Chinese" into English? Yet another erasure, folded doubly.

[3]

When I made it to the mainland, my uncle kept jabbing his elbow
at me as a map. We were in Zhuhai. His other hand made waves
around the elbow's shore. "The sea is everywhere," he said. "It's all
around us here." The water goes all the way north, to the snow, where
his granddaughter is in college. He kept mentioning the exciting
Hong Kong-Zhuhai-Macau Bridge project, which will be finished
by next year. Seen from the shore in Zhuhai, the Bridge is a thin
wire stretching through the mist, with occasional gaps for the mind
to fill. The construction of the Bridge, one of several ongoing white
elephant projects, has more to do with the Communist Party getting
in than with Hongkongers getting out; local taxpayers are giving up
billions to relinquish their city to a foreign machinery. Some see this
as another plank hoisted from the pirate ship, a step along the way
to sinking. Each unfinished gap in the Bridge already has a buttress
in place: pillars jutting out above the water. At present they look like
ruins.

The translation of "I Just Want to See the Sea" was accepted for
publication by a major international journal in English. A contract
was drawn up and signed. Then the editors changed their minds.
Buried in the rhetoric of their apology was this contradiction: first,
the topic was no longer timely; second, the essay's very timelessness,
that is to say its lyrical approach transcending Umbrella Stuff to speak
more broadly of Hong Kong and even more so of what it means to
be human, had too much of an insider's perspective. *Too much*. They
wanted a foreign gaze; they wanted a tour. The essay begins with a
writer going down to the sea during a painful political time, when
suddenly a security guard emerges to coax her back. What does it say
about this city on an island if the first assumption is that someone
sitting near water must want to throw herself in? And because of that
assumption, who is less free: her, or the guard?

The editors broke our contract and did not publish the essay, but they paid what they had promised to pay. After the fact, this felt like hush money. We talk so much about censorship in China, but there are silencings in every language along every sea. And we endure, and the enduring is not noble, and no one is listening.

I have stood on both sides of the water in one day. I can't see right from wrong anymore. I can walk you through injustices until the land ends, but I can't describe justice. Goethe said that to know is not enough; we have to act. But Gandhi said that none of us can know; none is competent to judge or act. How can we speak in an era whose censorship is not the blockage of information but the overloading of it, the white noise of privileged chatter?

Listen, I can't tell you what will be enough. All I've done is wipe dust from the pane. All I've left is my own thumbprint.

May we never forget the study corner in Admiralty, where solidarity was a kind of solitude: a space for private thought in the center of the throng. May we never forget those altars in Mong Kok which marked its topographic center. That was "Chapel Road," where the Kwan Tai altar faced the St. Francis Chapel on the Street: a space for prayer. May we hold dear the community libraries on styrofoam shelves in each of the three camps, which history will not remember when it swallows everyone's stories. On an English shelf in Admiralty was Anne Carson. In Causeway Bay was Kiran Desai. In Mong Kok was the Beckett trilogy: "Yes, in my life, since we must call it so, there were three things, the inability to speak, the inability to be silent, and solitude, that's what I've had to make the best of. . . . I wanted myself, in my own land for a brief space, I didn't want to die a stranger in the midst of strangers, a stranger in my own midst, surrounded by invaders . . ."

Let me tell you about the stranger in his early thirties who stood alone for a weekend in the Causeway Bay camp holding a yellow umbrella and a sign: "I do not support police violence." He had come from England four years ago, for work. A woman shouted at him across the barricade in English: "Go home! What right do you have? You are not Chinese. Go back to your country."

He said, "Thank you for your opinion."

She paused. She could not understand.

Then she resumed her shouting. Then he thanked her again.

He continued thanking her until some of us intervened to calm her down.

This, too, is not enough. But I give thanks for it anyway. Thank you for your being here. It is possible that none of us have the right to live as we do. That we are all of us always wrong, that this is the only premise on which real dialogue can be built. So thank you for standing alone. For your misunderstanding, for your pained cry. For this dust of words, for the longing to be at all, for we are all afraid in the end. Thank you, and thank you.

And then what? Then what?

IV

NEITHER SELF NOR NOT-SELF
NOR BOTH NOR NEITHER

(   )

:
:

                    Goddess of Democracy

                    "   "

        or

        "   "

            and
                    "   "

January   rain

67

You'd recognize me anywhere,
 you said. You'd mistake me
  for the ghost of my father.

  You'd wave.

  You jumped at this voice
like his voice, gene of accents
cleaving. I came to return

 the lost parcel of a tongue
  undelivered, a hair grayed
   and lifted by the storm

  that bore me here, lifted
like your home's brick face.
You removed your glasses

 and were beautiful, the mirror
  vanishing, the watches dead.

  You left before my birth.

  I came after revolution
 and refuge to speak, for all our grace,
of helplessness: every cry

 and eloquence is that.
  Every sorry, every thanks,

  and here I am.

  Did our village echo in the hall?
 Or was it just a broken pipe?
Did neighbors yell songs

 into the flood? We made it,
  most of us, made sumptuous

  a road without mail.

Your husband once sickled
            fields of anonymity
with my father.

        He crooked his hand
                to explain, then rubbed his eye,

                the scalpeled one,

            then asked who else
of mine had died.
Correction:

        you didn't forge my birth
                certificate, but the permit
                    for my birth.

            Correction:
        it was a two-child policy
for villagers, some mothers hidden

            in the bellies of mountains,
                with a valley between births
                    which you doctored.

            Correction: but the year
        I was born: correction:
stray cat subtracting

        from your door's cool bark;
                all of us opening inward.

                Correction: not most

            but some, some of us made it.
        Some became lantern rice:
hollow, infertile grains

        on stalks too slight to bend
                and nourishing no one.

                Correction: not hollow.

We set the table for dinner,
filled it with light. No, we set
altars. We set a soft fire.

ECHOCARDIOGRAMS

The images are made of sound. In every moment in the dark pockets inside us: tiny earthquakes. That's how music can shake up the ribcage, how cedar or spruce shaved down can shudder alive beneath strings of a matching tension. The wood cannot be said to sing, as the heart cannot be said to sing. Its vibrations are more like longing. In black and white on the monitor's screen, the heart is a toad whose face wipes away, whose arms are chained to the ceiling, who seizes from a heavy core, who goes nowhere. It looks like failed escape, or like heaving, or like laughter,

        this heart   this heart
              arrhythmic   heart-heart-heart.

If sound is spatial, then the arrangement of notes is neither language nor grammar. What lies between one note and the next? Absence, somatic. The heart inhales, the tremors pause. The screen goes dark. Every pulse is like a river chased back to its source, a gulping fist-sized misapprehension. Then the heart exhales. Seen from another angle, it's a puckered mouth, yelling. It's called the mitral valve, the small god of rocks, the gaping, giddy wound—

      gape   at me now
               what are we   now?

Even a leashed dog can mark a mute thing as territory. On systole, an egg can look whole, only to crack again on diastole. I keep meaning to arrive on the plane that went missing before my birth. Breastplates of ice peel from the drain grates. There is no life after nationhood, no tombolo at high tide. Every inside is a dark moss, a damaged, unspeakable face. We speak of darkness at far edges where light can't reach, but darkness is behind each light too. It's an octave rubbing its back against the end of the line. Can a ghostlight exist in us, as on every blank theater stage? The dead of night, the artifice, the portal:

      and I am   and no one
           an outline   outlying

Your mother rubs her whipping arm.
To punish is to be divine.

The Romans used to say: "*Amabo te*,"
Which means, "I love you." Or: "Please."

Encounter this.

Limb of a creek longing for water for years —
Deaf ghost wearing weariness like a shield —

You bloom in this world to be benign
As a tumor, a scribble on the inner void.

Be outer lining, too.

Your cry is what makes her whipping arm numb.
You are a fence outlining two homes.

Be algebra: where x is holiness, holes,
The cat in the box. Be variable.

Be all, and broken.

Know: your mother dove into the sea
To never return, hung from a balcony

And lived. You face a saved body,
A *machinus ex dei*, a rewired flesh.

Be studious to her death.

DIRGE FOR THE GODDESS

On 8 Feb 2016, groups forged in the failed Umbrella Movement rallied to resist police brutality against unlicensed hawkers, particularly where one of the Occupy encampments had been.

The showdown became Hong Kong's first riot in fifty years.

Your statue hand
reaches for mine.

It is eternity
we must endure.

"Abandon all hope"—
you know the rest—

but you always said:
hope *with* abandon,

be passion renouncing
even itself.

A spider descends
from your caverned eye

to your wrist and chin
where flies persist

embalmed.
You've lost fingers.

Something ribbons in me,
my deepest rivers.

I will forget your name.

And you, who studied
an abysmal grace,

will become inner
tree bark, smooth

as doors, wiser
than longing.

Tell me again
how you descended once

with holy doves
in your breath

and no happier
than before.

Tell me: have I left
loved ones to die?

Tell me there's no
fearlessness,

only more
precise fears.

STILL LIFE AT AN ATROCITY CAMP

Here the birds thrive.
Swallow droppings
stain the mats,
scribble the walls.
Footsteps in a tunnel,
a sound like chewed rocks.
Skylight, dim circle.
To stand in a beam
of light is not to know
the light, only
glass, veins of dirt.
Brick prison, window,
across the moat
another brick window
and a far door
opening inward.
In the river,
twenty-two thousand
were made ash
and emptied
without names.
Now fish jump
so often the dust
won't settle.
Now a golf course
winds the bend
where men haul
wheeled black bags
as large as bodies.
A fallen pear
splits open,
green flap pulled free
by a fist of bees
beside their dead queen.

QUARANTINE

My feet pound perimeters
into the earth, and I grow old
while the long, imperceptible curve
of the city cuts ahead of me
like a ledge. In the last one
billion years, the moon shrank
a little. Pain travels through me
at three hundred feet per second:
missives for a traitor well loved.
My suitcase wheels clack over
every square of sidewalk.
Mountains heave up; I can walk
over anything if I don't stop.
My lungs won't fill with stems.
During the Black Death, ships
were kept apart in harbors
for forty days, never more.

SON I'LL NEVER HAVE

I'd abandon you
for the old pond any day,
fix my posture by a sun
dialing shadows on the surface
without numbers.

I'd give you, my soul,
and each salvific hunger
in exchange for windmills
whipping like breaths barely
held beyond the trees.
I'd burn this country
with you in it

and salt the earth,
to go on thinking without cease
that here the tallest tree
is me: that thin, tumorous
evergreen whose elbows tremble
over the remains of winter.

It's no more dead than the deciduous.
Its loneliness cannot be known.

Not even undone nests can cry,
not for all the world's springs.

For canopies of hair and fingernail,
for momentary fish, for less than this,
I'd feed you to the dry and hush,
the thirst, the vanished line, the absence, whole.

I'd do all this and more and see
what lasting holiness
your way recedes. If peace
were transmitted
like a disease, you'd know me
finally, sitting here: a young empire,
robbed and sighing, holding one last die.

FATHER EMPIRE

You left a sack of quick-concrete
against the tree downstairs.
It didn't rot like our potatoes,
nor ooze like worming rice.

The rains came; the sack hardened.
The rains went; the sack bled off.
Only concrete remained, stood
like grave shoulders barely upright,

rock without language, immutable
upon the roots. Meanwhile: leaves.
Meanwhile: elbows lifting, naked,
to the cold. Meanwhile: winged seeds.

When I became a man, I found your jacket
springing in snow, creamy wool long
become flesh, outer sheen a shell,
abandoned thing of sleeves which didn't fit.

I hung it from a branch. Wind filled the hood,
and hanged it.
                    Haven't I paid my way?
I paid my way without you.

I wrenched the hands off our clocks,
I listened to the tongues still clucking.
You only left us with time this time.
You proved that fiction is a form of worry.

You are a form of worry.
One of us was always meant to be
an ocean: unrequiting, distant,
deafening the ear at its chest.

STRUGGLE AFTER THE WOMB

Why wrestle any angel
before daybreak?   *A riddle.*

A poet said it's our triumph
to lose: to be mutilated at the hinge
by a blessed knowing.

Shore of the shell of the thing
we call home — the shore endures.

*Can we map inner life
without erasure?*

A saint said it's our tragedy
to lose yet stay standing:
before God, to fail to be extinguished.

A map is an erasure.

A pillar of birdseed said:
Lest I die let me die
that I may see —

*Best to keep crossing
the river. Tell no one
what you saw and held.
Your angels ruin us.*

Let the body prove it's capable
of hardness all it wants — a shore
endures — look, your heart meets its
parenthesis
but says: then what?   then what?

Then sunrise dangles its limb
from the sky's gray heft.

And then you part ways
as water parts a way,
collapsible, concave.

ISLAND OF THE GODDESS

*On 29 Feb 2016, a student leader in the riot ran in a by-election for the Legislative
Council. He lost by a slim margin, but his radical campaign opened a conversation
about Hong Kong's independence from China.*

Ask me what I left for you.
I became by becoming empty.
I left small gods of noise,
entered a wood, never stopped flying.
I left you by a light so near
annihilation you pressed your dark
skin against a wall, peeling.

A wall is a sieve.
You said: *Isn't this all?*
We solve what's divine, God leaves us
limping, we mistake thanks
for love? Ask me why I left you
all this love, whole
kingdoms of useless salt.

I turned course long ago
by a shrug of the shoulders
while our flock went on,
an inarticulate dot
among dots, an impossible
gene, impossible exile,
calling out: fly!

By this time next year
I'll have no more face.
No more surface.

(Isn't every goodbye mortal?
Wasn't ours a life of postcards
with no person in them?)

One day, I'll face the truth.

But if the truth excludes you,
let me face you.

"OPEN HEART," OR HAPPINESS TRANSLATED AS "WOUND"

You must feel this ineloquence
of me: stale enclosure,
my translated being being translated.
What dies, in each word, to feed us?

      Precision is the only mercy.
          Wildflowers sugaring a field—

Is it true what they say,
that having makes a hole?
I have not gladness enough
for such a loss. I repent having.

      Zeno said it: motion indivisible.
          Flinging eggshells at garden soil—

Or was it halving that makes whole?
Every road halfway, every halfway
halved. We pack up but never move.
I halve the first Linzertorte. We eat it forever.

      A storm carries the cusp of closeness.
          Split tongues spilt rain mercied into sea—

Weren't we coals which some mouth burned?
Erase me, find me. Re-render these words
as a pond. Rend every surface as light.
Is it enough to stay here in silence—

      Between our survivings is a lost space—
          To say this with silence? January rain.

It's not the way you rend
and unpeople me. It's not how

I try being your church
but erect steeples instead.

It's not the room without object,
the whole and unsayable,
uncurtained.

Not the caverned tide.

Not how we're broken,
hair's breadth from a mend,
a mean mistaken for life;

not how houseplants grow dust
without us, how sometimes

there's no one. It's not love

as mnemonic, not love

as not enough, not love

made onomatopoetic.
It's not this sick gladness.

Not the shallow well,
nor my secret opening in it.

No, it's this inspired fear
of a life without you—

      but what can I know
        of *with*?

Just clumsy tennisball days;
a clock; a cleft. A country

cleared of all beds; and no exit.

SHELLS IN THE SOIL

There was a burying of plants.
I sought cover, not knowing the rain
was only wind shuddering through leaves.
If I become the light, I will only seem
to move, but will not move,
while an oak fern closes its fingers
and I fill its hollow palm. I ask
to remain unmarked;

I am an island
blooming rust.

The rain has stopped.
Dear mayapple, your umbrella is burnt.
I see your veins from below. You alone
are browning here (a robin trills with twigs
wreathed in its beak, a fly treads water
in terrible calm), and I thank your folding
like a wet flag: may your dying
always grant us shade.

INDEPENDENCE CREED: AN AMENDMENT

I believe the letters
("these are the most important letters
I write," says R, "letters like the alphabet")

in this box are all you'll know me by.
I leave nothing else. Believe me,
I was no more than a hopeful

ideal reader my loved ones imagined
in the night. I never sought happiness
("you're sad," says D, "aren't you,

and you've been training yourself
to play this life only to play it well")
but I've found, in language, in this game

of symbols drawn from some desire's shore
such a vast love that in every writing
I believe I sight the other in me,

the better, the perfect object
("you're a coward," says B)
("you're a con artist," says B's ex before me)

which I might leave behind; remember
me this way. I believe there's no wrong
in being loved more than I can love

("but somehow I feel," says Q,
"a better home with you") although
it means housing a new loneliness.

I believe in night whispers like fog
and foundering, I believe in bodies
opening windows, in umbrellas

opening statues. I believe in you. I believe
you'll write soon ("no good reason," says F,
"for why it's been so hard to write")

and I'll sit by the mailbox knowing
something has changed, has come
into being but hasn't arrived; your words

are late. They're too late to save me.
Yet every line is some salvation
("something, always," says K,

"consoling about these letters")
so what's it matter *for whom?*
Believe I meant to do more before

all this: although I never said bye, I
believe in goodbyes ("Teacher Chickenhead,"
says N, "be save, and come back soon").

I believe in flags evaporating
like fields of ice under sudden heat,
which is just to say "how many times

in life you grow close to people and then
have to leave them" (M); I believe "I'm glad
we've kept in touch" (S) after my treasons.

I believe the you who reads this is the same
who placed a turtle in my box to say:
carry your home on your back. It weighs

on my words. I'll thank you one day
for your words (for *your* words)
though it won't be enough, it will sound

like an apology, like the no-longer sticky note
on a birthday letter sent here seven months late—
"obviously the relevance of this diminishes

by the minute"—and I know, each year
when I weep for this nation of words, *I know,*
the line needs my faith, needs a creed

built from what it, and we, could never be.

ENVOI AT LOW TIDE

(ABRIDGED TIMELINE: HONG KONG 2014)

June 4: Tiananmen Massacre Memorial Vigil
June 10: Beijing releases White Paper emphasizing Hong Kong's dependence

July 1: Anniversary protest of 1997 Handover

August 31: Beijing announces bogus universal suffrage for Hong Kong
: "Occupy Central with Love and Peace" rally

September 4: Student strike discussed at Goddess of Democracy statue at Chinese University
September 22-26: Student strike
September 26-27: Students climb fence into Civic Square, arrested for sit-in
: Protests multiply
September 28: Tear gas launched at protesters using umbrellas as shields
: Commencement of "Umbrella Revolution/Movement"
: Admiralty, Mong Kok, Causeway Bay occupied

October 2: Commencement of Mobile Democracy Classroom in each protest camp
October 3: Unchecked violence against protesters in Mong Kok begins
October 8: Study Corner built in Admiralty
October 11: Guan Yu altar built in Mong Kok
October 13: St Francis Chapel on the Street built in Mong Kok
October 14: Police brutality caught on film at Lung Wo Road near PLA garrison
October 17: Mong Kok cleared by police in early morning
: Mong Kok reoccupied by protesters at midnight
October 21 : Government dialogue with students
: No concessions
October 23: "I want genuine universal suffrage" banner hung from Lion Rock peak

November 5: Anonymous thousand masks march, face-off with police at Lung Wo Road
November 8: Pride Parade converges in Admiralty
November 9: Legislative Council windows smashed, protest groups splinter
November 25-26: Crackdown and demolition of Mong Kok the agon
: Commencement of Mobile Occupy, or "Shopping Revolution"
November 30: Lung Wo Road occupied and lost
: Police threaten to rape female protesters in station

December 11: Demolition of Admiralty the agora, with mass arrests
December 15: Demolition of Causeway Bay the orpheum
December 24: Fourteen-year-old girl detained for drawing chalk flowers beside umbrella symbol

(January 6: Hong Kong government releases bogus report on protests to Beijing)
(January 19: Hong Kong Army Cadets established for training patriotic youth)

Who can believe in words wrested free of things?
Isn't he a fool who tries writing you to freedom?

Your name, once, for me, inked on your palm;
That morning, a fist closing, opening, a free end.

Sometimes closeness is the bridge unhinging.
Salmon shudder into wild nets, widely, freely.

I never meant to be this kind of ghost, holding,
Out of sequence, your secret freedoms.

The truth is like time: a zone alive in the body —
And words: as light as death, too feathered, too free.

Good monster of the lungs, lead the way...
Electric bare forest freer than fear's fiefdom...

* You are a full silence I cannot redeem. You need
No breath from me, not on your life. Not for your freedom.

ACKNOWLEDGMENTS

Many thanks to the editors of the following journals for publishing earlier versions of these poems, often under different titles: *Asian American Literary Review*: "Sonnet for the Goddess," "Preamble: Room for Cadavers," "Father Empire," "'Open Heart' or Happiness Translated As 'Wound'"; *Berkeley Poetry Review*: "Still Life at an Atrocity Camp"; *Blueshift Journal*: "Island of the Goddess" (When did I leave...); *Cha*: "Disobedience," "Island of the Goddess" (What they meant...), "Shells in the Soil," "Dedication Endnote"; *The Collagist*: "Independence Creed: An Amendment"; Drunken Boat: "Ruins Above Water"; *Dusie*: "Victims of Communism Memorial"; *Hawai'i Independent*: "Translation Poem for Hong Kong"; *Hawai'i Review*: "Island of the Goddess" (Ask me what...); *Kartika Review*: "Quarantine"; *Puerto del Sol*: "Meeting the Woman Who Forged My Birth Certificate," "Goods of Democracy"; *Spillway*: "Archery For a Future Daughter"; *Wasafiri*: "Dear Exile," "An Umbrella: Revolution," "An Umbrella: Movement." My gratitude to editors Tammy Ho, Susan Terris, and Gerald Maa for the Pushcart nominations.

The epigraphs come from Simone Weil's *Waiting for God* and Samuel Beckett's *The Unnamable*. "Lest I die let me die that I may see" is cut from the Chadwick rendering of St. Augustine's "moriar, ne moriar, ut eam videam." "Independence Creed" is in homage to a poem by Meg Kearney.

Parts of this manuscript were completed on the sly during time paid for by the Paul & Daisy Soros Fellowship for New Americans, the Helen Zell Post-MFA Fellowship, and the William J. Fulbright Fellowship, and under the support of the Kundiman Fellowship.

This book is for the cage, and for the caged ones who stand up anyway.

photo: Lo Mei Wa

Henry Wei Leung was born in the Pearl River Delta and raised in
Honolulu and the San Francisco Bay Area. He earned his BA from
Stanford, then his MFA in Fiction from the Helen Zell Writers'
Program, and has been the recipient of Kundiman, Soros, and
Fulbright Fellowships. He is the author of a chapbook, *Paradise
Hunger* (Swan Scythe, 2012), and the translator of Wawa's *Pei Pei the
Monkey King* (Tinfish, 2016). In addition to his creative and editorial
work, he has written culture reviews for such magazines as *TimeOut
Hong Kong* and *ArtAsiaPacific*. He recently dropped out of a PhD
program to spend some time farming with his wife on the island of
Keawe.

Goddess of Democracy: an Occupy lyric
by Henry Wei Leung

Cover image: *Absent of Speech*, Yip Kin Bon, 2014/2015,
190 x 120 cm, newspaper. www.yipkinbon.com

Cover and interior set in Kabel LT Std and Didot LT Std
Chinese characters set in Menlo and Apple LiSung

Cover and interior design by Gillian Olivia Blythe Hamel

Offset printed in the United States
by Edwards Brothers Malloy, Ann Arbor, Michigan
On 55# Enviro Natural 100% Recycled 100% PCW
Acid Free Archival Quality FSC Certified Paper

Publication of this book was made possible in part by gifts from:
The Clorox Company
The New Place Fund
Robin & Curt Caton

Omnidawn Publishing
Oakland, California
2017

Rusty Morrison & Ken Keegan, senior editors & co-publishers
Gillian Olivia Blythe Hamel, managing editor
Cassandra Smith, poetry editor & book designer
Sharon Zetter, poetry editor, book designer & development officer
Avren Keating, poetry editor, fiction editor & marketing assistant
Liza Flum, poetry editor
Juliana Paslay, fiction editor
Gail Aronson, fiction editor
Trisha Peck, marketing assistant
Cameron Stuart, marketing assistant
Natalia Cinco, marketing assistant
Maria Kosiyanenko, marketing assistant
Emma Thomason, administrative assistant
SD Sumner, copyeditor
Kevin Peters, *OmniVerse* Lit Scene editor
Sara Burant, *OmniVerse* reviews editor